Obama, In His Own Words:
Pre-Election

Carl "Tuchy" Palmieri

ISBN: 1-4392-2608-3
ISBN-13: 9781439226087

Visit www.booksurge.com to order additional copies.

To my dad, who came to America as a 15-year-old. He attended night school while working to make a new life. Dad was proud to be a citizen; grateful for the opportunity to work and earn a living. Dad lived a life believing that America was the best country in the world, knowing that he was free to do or be almost everything in the U.S., the only exception being that of President of the United States. Dad passed away in 1992 at the age of 78 and from all measures, died a successful man.

To my wonderful wife, Susan, who encourages me each and every day to bring happiness and satisfaction to my success and to enjoy the journey.

To our wonderful children—Kathleen, Phil, Amy, John, and Stephen.

To our amazing grandchildren—Sean, Alicia, Heather, Julia, Olivia, C.J., Jack, Will, Tiny II (Julia), Ava, Chris, Sophia, and Adeline—and to all our loved ones.

OBAMA, IN HIS WORDS

1) "A good compromise, a good piece of legislation, is like a good sentence or a good piece of music. Everybody can recognize it. They say, 'Huh. It works. It makes sense.'"

2) "If the people cannot trust their government to do the job for which it exists—to protect them and to promote their common welfare—all else is lost."

3) "What Washington needs is adult supervision."

4) "Most people who serve in Washington have been trained either as lawyers or as political operatives—professions that tend to place a premium on winning arguments rather than solving problems."

5) "In Africa, you often see that the difference between a village where everybody eats and a village where people starve is government. One has a functioning government and the other does not. Which is why it bothers me when I hear people say that government is the enemy."

THE PEOPLE

What I appreciate about my country is:

_____

_____

What I love about my state is:

_____

_____

What I am grateful for about my city/town is:

_____

_____

What I am joyful about my family/fellowship/friends is:

_____

_____

What I acknowledge for myself is:

_____

_____

The action I am willing to take today for my country/state/city/
town/family/fellowship/friends/myself is

_____

_____

THE PEOPLE

1) "Americans still believe in an America where anything's possible—they just don't think their leaders do."

2) "Change will not come if we wait for some other person or some other time. We are the ones we've been waiting for. We are the change that we seek."

3) "Focusing your life solely on making a buck shows a certain poverty of ambition. It asks too little of yourself. Because it's only when you hitch your wagon to something larger than yourself that you realize your true potential."

4) "Faith doesn't mean that you don't have doubts."

5) "Yes, our greatness as a nation has depended on individual initiative; on a belief in the free market. But it has also depended on our sense of mutual regard for each other, of mutual responsibility. The idea that everybody has a stake in the country, that we're all in it together and everybody's got a shot at opportunity. Americans know this. We know that government can't solve all our problems—and we don't want it to. But we also know that there are some things we can't do on our own. We know that there are some things we do better together."

THE PEOPLE

What I appreciate about my country is:

_____

_____

What I love about my state is:

_____

_____

What I am grateful for about my city/town is:

_____

_____

What I am joyful about my family/fellowship/friends is:

_____

_____

What I acknowledge for myself is:

_____

_____

The action I am willing to take today for my country/state/city/town/family/fellowship/friends/myself is:

_____

_____

THE PEOPLE—CONTINUED

6) "Making your mark on the world is hard. If it were easy, everybody would do it. But it's not. It takes patience, it takes commitment, and it comes with plenty of failure along the way. The real test is not whether you avoid this failure, because you won't. It's whether you let it harden or shame you into inaction, or whether you learn from it; whether you choose to persevere."

7) "If we aren't willing to pay a price for our values, then we should ask ourselves whether we truly believe in them at all."

8) "Faith is not just something you have, it's something you do."

9) "We have a stake in one another. What binds us together is greater than what drives us apart and if enough people believe in the truth of that proposition and act on it, then we might not solve every problem, but we can get something meaningful done for the people with whom we share this Earth."

10) "It's only when you hitch your wagon to something larger than yourself that you will realize your true potential."

11) "What I think I found in the American people, I think there's a core decency there, where if they take the time, if they get the time to know individuals, then they want to judge those individuals by their character."

THE PEOPLE

What I appreciate about my country is:

_____

_____

What I love about my state is:

_____

_____

What I am grateful for about my city/town is:

_____

_____

What I am joyful about my family/fellowship/friends is:

_____

_____

What I acknowledge for myself is:

_____

_____

The action I am willing to take today for my country/state/city/
town/family/fellowship/friends/myself is:

_____

_____

THE PEOPLE—CONTINUED

12) "Spend time actually talking to Americans and you discover that most evangelicals are more tolerant than the media would have us believe, and most secularists more spiritual. Most rich people want the poor to succeed, and most of the poor are both more self-critical and hold higher aspirations than the popular culture allows."

13) "I think that we still have prejudice in our midst but I think that the vast majority of Americans are willing to judge people on the basis of, you know, their ideas and their character."

14) "What I've found is that the American people—once they get to know you—are going to judge you on your individual character. Whatever the flaws in the process, people get a fairly accurate read by the end of the campaign."

15) "We will remember that we are not as divided as our politics suggests; that we are one people; we are one nation and together, we will begin the next great chapter in the American story with three words that will ring from coast to coast, from sea to shining sea: Yes. We. Can."

16) "As Americans, we can take enormous pride in the fact that courage has been inspired by our own struggle for freedom, by the tradition of democratic law secured by our forefathers and enshrined in our Constitution. It is a tradition that says all men are created equal under the law and that no one is above it."

ON PRESIDENTS

What I appreciate about my country is:

_____

_____

What I love about my state is:

_____

_____

What I am grateful for about my city/town is:

_____

_____

What I am joyful about my family/fellowship/friends is:

_____

_____

What I acknowledge for myself is:

_____

_____

The action I am willing to take today for my country/state/city/town/family/fellowship/friends/myself is:

_____

_____

ON PRESIDENTS

1) "I cannot swallow whole the view of Lincoln as the Great Emancipator."

2) "Hillary is not the first politician in Washington to declare 'Mission Accomplished' a little too soon."

ON ABORTION

1) "I've got two daughters; nine years old and six years old. I am going to teach them first of all about values and morals. But if they make a mistake, I don't want them punished with a baby."

2) "No one is pro-abortion."

ON BEING THE BEST YOU CAN BE

What I appreciate about my country is:

_____

_____

What I love about my state is:

_____

_____

What I am grateful for about my city/town is:

_____

_____

What I am joyful about my family/fellowship/friends is:

_____

_____

What I acknowledge for myself is:

_____

_____

The action I am willing to take today for my country/state/city/
town/family/fellowship/friends/myself is:

_____

_____

ON BEING THE BEST YOU CAN BE

1) "If you're walking down the right path and you're willing to keep walking, eventually you'll make progress."

2) "It took a lot of blood, sweat, and tears to get to where we are today, but we have just begun. Today we begin in earnest the work of making sure that the world we leave our children is just a little bit better than the one we inhabit today."

3) "We need to internalize this idea of excellence. Not many folks spend a lot of time trying to be excellent."

4) "We need to steer clear of this poverty of ambition, where people want to drive fancy cars and wear nice clothes and live in nice apartments but don't want to work hard to accomplish these things."

5) "Everyone should try to realize their full potential "

6) "Life doesn't count for much unless you're willing to do your small part to leave our children—all of our children—a better world. Even if it's difficult. Even if the work seems great. Even if we don't get very far in our lifetime."

ON THE ISSUES/ON MONEY

What I appreciate about my country is

_____

_____

What I love about my state is:

_____

_____

What I am grateful for about my city/town is:

_____

_____

What I am joyful about my family/fellowship/friends is:

_____

_____

What I acknowledge for myself is:

_____

_____

The action I am willing to take today for my country/state/city/
town/family/fellowship/friends/myself is:

_____

_____

ON THE ISSUES

1) "Issues are never simple. One thing I am proud of is that very rarely will you hear me simplify the issues."

ON MONEY

1) "Money is not the only answer, but it makes a difference."

2) "I think the problem of money in politics is bipartisan. I think that all of us who are involved in the political process have to be concerned about the enormous sums of money that have to be raised in order to run campaigns, how that money's raised, and at least the appearance of impropriety and the potential access that's given to those who are contributing. That's a general problem with our politics. The specific problem of inviting lobbyists in who have bundled huge sums of money to write legislation, having the oil and gas companies come in to write energy legislation, having drug companies come in and write the Medicare prescription drug bill—which we now see is not working for our seniors—those are very particular problems of this administration and this Congress. And I think Jack Abramoff and the K Street Project, that whole thing is a very particular Republican sin."

ON OBAMA'S STAND

What I appreciate about my country is:

_____

_____

What I love about my state is:

_____

_____

What I am grateful for about my city/town is:

_____

_____

What I am joyful about my family/fellowship/friends is:

_____

_____

What I acknowledge for myself is:

_____

_____

The action I am willing to take today for my country/state/city/
town/family/fellowship/friends/myself is:

_____

_____

ON OBAMA'S STAND

1) "My job is not to represent Washington to you, but to represent you to Washington."

2) "The fact that my 15 minutes of fame has extended a little longer than 15 minutes is somewhat surprising to me and completely baffling to my wife."

3) "We need somebody who's got the heart, the empathy, to recognize what it's like to be a young teenage mom; the empathy to understand what it's like to be poor or African-American or gay or disabled or old—and that's the criterion by which I'll be selecting my judges."

4) "Our law is by definition a codification of morality, much of it grounded in the Judeo-Christian tradition."

5) "To say that men and women should not inject their 'personal morality' into public policy debates is a practical absurdity."

ON OBAMA'S STAND

What I appreciate about my country is:

_____

_____

What I love about my state is:

_____

_____

What I am grateful for about my city/town is:

_____

_____

What I am joyful about my family/fellowship/friends is:

_____

_____

What I acknowledge for myself is:

_____

_____

The action I am willing to take today for my country/state/city/
town/family/fellowship/friends/myself is:

_____

_____

ON OBAMA'S STAND—CONTINUED

6) "I believe in keeping guns out of our inner cities, and that our leaders must say so in the face of the gun manufacturer's lobby. But I also believe that when a gang-banger shoots indiscriminately into a crowd because he feels someone disrespected him, we have a problem of morality. Not only do we need to punish that man for his crime, but we need to acknowledge that there's a hole in his heart, one that government programs alone may not be able to repair."

7) "We've gotta restore the American people's confidence in the ethics process by ensuring that political self-interest can no longer prevent politicians from enforcing ethics rules."

8) "To curb the spread of nuclear weapons and ensure that the American people know where their tax dollars are being spent, and to reduce the influence of lobbyists who have all too often set the agenda in Washington. In our country, I have found that this cooperation happens not because we agree on everything, but because behind all the false labels and false divisions and categories that define us; beyond all the petty bickering and point-scoring in Washington, Americans are a decent, generous, compassionate people, united by common challenges and common hopes. And every so often, there are moments which call on that fundamental goodness to make this country great again."

9) "I honor—we honor—the service of John McCain, and I respect his many accomplishments, even if he chooses to deny mine."

10) "I don't have a litmus test, but I do expect that there's a core of constitutional values that are going to be upheld in these next series of appointments, and I suspect that I will have something to say about who's going to shape the legal landscape for the next forty or fifty years."

ON AMERICA

What I appreciate about my country is:

_____

_____

What I love about my state is:

_____

_____

What I am grateful for about my city/town is:

_____

_____

What I am joyful about my family/fellowship/friends is:

_____

_____

What I acknowledge for myself is:

_____

_____

The action I am willing to take today for my country/state/city/town/family/fellowship/friends/myself is:

_____

_____

ON AMERICA

1) "My parents shared not only an improbable love, they shared an abiding faith in the possibilities of this nation. They would give me an African name, Barack, or blessed, believing that in a tolerant America your name is no barrier to success."

2) "There is not a liberal America and a conservative America—there is the United States of America. There is not a black America and a white America and Latino America and Asian America—there's the United States of America."

3) "There's not a liberal America and a conservative America—there's the United States of America."

4) "Tonight, we gather to affirm the greatness of our nation—not because of the height of our skyscrapers, or the power of our military, or the size of our economy. Our pride is based on a very simple premise, summed up in a declaration made over two hundred years ago."

5) "That is the true genius of America, a faith in the simple dreams of its people; the insistence on small miracles."

6) "We can say what we think, write what we think, without hearing a sudden knock on the door."

ON AMERICA

What I appreciate about my country is:

_____

_____

What I love about my state is:

_____

_____

What I am grateful for about my city/town is:

_____

_____

What I am joyful about my family/fellowship/friends is:

_____

_____

What I acknowledge for myself is:

_____

_____

The action I am willing to take today for my country/state/city/
town/family/fellowship/friends/myself is:

_____

_____

ON AMERICA—CONTINUED

7) "That we can have an idea and start our own business without paying a bribe or hiring somebody's son."

8) "We can participate in the political process without fear of retribution, and that our votes will be counted—or at least, most of the time."

9) "The true test of the American ideal is whether we're able to recognize our failings and then rise together to meet the challenges of our time. Whether we allow ourselves to be shaped by events and history, or whether we act to shape them."

10) "America is a land of big dreamers and big hopes. It is this hope that has sustained us through revolution and civil war, depression and world war, a struggle for civil and social rights and the brink of nuclear crisis. And it is because our dreamers dreamed that we have emerged from each challenge more united, more prosperous, and more admired than before."

11) "I always believe that ultimately, if people are paying attention, then we get good government and good leadership. And when we get lazy as a democracy and civically start taking shortcuts, then it results in bad government and politics."

12) "This union may never be perfect, but generation after generation has shown that it can always be perfected."

ON EDUCATION/SLIP-UPS

What I appreciate about my country is:

_____

_____

What I love about my state is:

_____

_____

What I am grateful for about my city/town is:

_____

_____

What I am joyful about my family/fellowship/friends is:

_____

_____

What I acknowledge for myself is:

_____

_____

The action I am willing to take today for my country/state/city/
town/family/fellowship/friends/myself is:

_____

_____

ON EDUCATION

1) "We have an obligation and a responsibility to be investing in our students and our schools. We must make sure that people who have the grades, the desire, and the will, but not the money, can still get the best education possible."

2) "With the changing economy, no one has lifetime employment. But community colleges provide lifetime employability."

SLIP-UPS

1) "Over the last 15 months, we've traveled to every corner of the United States. I've now been in 57 states? I think one left to go."

2) "I did. It's not something that I'm proud of. It was a mistake as a young man, but you know? I mean not going to—I never understood that line. The point was to inhale. That was the point."

SLIP-UPS

What I appreciate about my country is:

_____

_____

What I love about my state is:

_____

_____

What I am grateful for about my city/town is:

_____

_____

What I am joyful about my family/fellowship/friends is:

_____

_____

What I acknowledge for myself is:

_____

_____

The action I am willing to take today for my country/state/city/
town/family/fellowship/friends/myself is:

_____

_____

SLIP-UPS—CONTINUED

3) "I had learned not to care. I blew a few smoke rings, remembering those years. Pot had helped, and booze; maybe a little blow when you could afford it. Not smack, though..."

—Barack Obama, admitting taking cannabis and cocaine as a teenager, in 1995 memoir <u>Dreams from My Father</u>.

4) "'Junkie. Pothead.' That's where I'd been headed: the final, fatal role of the young would-be black man. Except the highs hadn't been about that; me trying to prove what a down brother I was. Not by then, anyway. I got high for just the opposite effect; something that could push questions of who I was out of my mind, something that could flatten out the landscape of my heart, blur the edges of my memory. I had discovered that it didn't make any difference whether you smoked reefer in the white classmate's sparkling new van, or in the dorm room of some brother you'd met down at the gym, or on the beach with a couple of Hawaiian kids who had dropped out of school and now spent most of their time looking for an excuse to brawl... You might just be bored, or alone. Everybody was welcome into the club of disaffection."

5) "It was usually an effective tactic; another one of those tricks I had learned: (White) people were satisfied so long as you were courteous and smiled and made no sudden moves. They were more than satisfied, they were relieved—such a pleasant surprise to find a well-mannered young black man who didn't seem angry all the time."

ON THE WAR ON TERROR

What I appreciate about my country is:

_____

_____

What I love about my state is:

_____

_____

What I am grateful for about my city/town is:

_____

_____

What I am joyful about my family/fellowship/friends is:

_____

_____

What I acknowledge for myself is:

_____

_____

The action I am willing to take today for my country/state/city/town/family/fellowship/friends/myself is:

_____

_____

ON THE WAR ON TERROR

1) "Operations in Iraq and Afghanistan and the war on terrorism have reduced the pace of military transformation and have revealed our lack of preparation for defensive and stability operations."

2) "There are patriots who opposed the war in Iraq and there are patriots who supported the war in Iraq. We are one people, all of us pledging allegiance to the stars and stripes, all of us defending the United States of America."

3) "Today we are engaged in a deadly global struggle for those who would intimidate, torture, and murder people for exercising the most basic freedoms. If we are to win this struggle and spread those freedoms, we must keep our own moral compass pointed in a true direction."

4) "We have real enemies in the world. These enemies must be found. They must be pursued and they must be defeated."

5) "We're not going to baby-sit a civil war."

ON THE WAR ON TERROR

What I appreciate about my country is:

_____

_____

What I love about my state is:

_____

_____

What I am grateful for about my city/town is:

_____

_____

What I am joyful about my family/fellowship/friends is:

_____

_____

What I acknowledge for myself is:

_____

_____

The action I am willing to take today for my country/state/city/
town/family/fellowship/friends/myself is:

_____

_____

ON THE WAR ON TERROR—CONTINUED

6) "Where the stakes are the highest, in the war on terror, we cannot possibly succeed without extraordinary international cooperation. Effective international police actions require the highest degree of intelligence sharing, planning, and collaborative enforcement."

7) "In an interconnected world, the defeat of international terrorism—and most importantly, the prevention of these terrorist organizations from obtaining weapons of mass destruction—will require the cooperation of many nations. We must always reserve the right to strike unilaterally at terrorists wherever they may exist. But we should know that our success in doing so is enhanced by engaging our allies so that we receive the crucial diplomatic, military, intelligence, and financial support that can lighten our load and add legitimacy to our actions. This means talking to our friends and, at times, even our enemies."

8) "We should be more modest in our belief that we can impose democracy on a country through military force."

9) "In the past, it has been movements for freedom from within tyrannical regimes that have led to flourishing democracies; movements that continue today. This doesn't mean abandoning our values and ideals; wherever we can, it's in our interest to help foster democracy through the diplomatic and economic resources at our disposal. But even as we provide such help, we should be clear that the institutions of democracy—free markets, a free press, a strong civil society—cannot be built overnight, and they cannot be built at the end of a barrel of a gun."

ON THE WAR ON TERROR

What I appreciate about my country is:

_____

_____

What I love about my state is:

_____

_____

What I am grateful for about my city/town is:

_____

_____

What I am joyful about my family/fellowship/friends is:

_____

_____

What I acknowledge for myself is:

_____

_____

The action I am willing to take today for my country/state/city/town/family/fellowship/friends/myself is:

_____

_____

ON THE WAR ON TERROR—CONTINUED

10) "And so we must realize that the freedoms FDR once spoke of—especially freedom from want and freedom from fear—do not just come from deposing a tyrant and handing out ballots; they are only realized once the personal and material security of a people is ensured as well."

11) "When we send our young men and women into harm's way, we have a solemn obligation not to fudge the numbers or shade the truth about why they're going; to care for their families while they're gone; to tend to the soldiers upon their return; and to never ever go to war without enough troops to win the war, secure the peace, and earn the respect of the world."

12) "Our enemies are fully aware that they can use oil as a weapon against America. And if we don't take this threat as seriously as the bombs they build or the guns they buy, we will be fighting the War on Terror with one hand tied behind our back."

13) "In the end, no amount of American forces can solve the political differences that lie at the heart of somebody else's civil war."

ON THE WAR ON TERROR

What I appreciate about my country is:

_____

_____

What I love about my state is:

_____

_____

What I am grateful for about my city/town is:

_____

_____

What I am joyful about my family/fellowship/friends is:

_____

_____

What I acknowledge for myself is:

_____

_____

The action I am willing to take today for my country/state/city/
town/family/fellowship/friends/myself is:

_____

_____

ON THE WAR ON TERROR—CONTINUED

14) "There is no military solution to the war in Iraq. Our troops can help suppress the violence, but they cannot solve its root causes. And all the troops in the world won't be able to force Shia, Sunni, and Kurd to sit down at a table, resolve their differences, and forge a lasting peace. In fact, adding more troops will only push this political settlement further and further into the future, as it tells the Iraqis that no matter how much of a mess they make, the American military will always be there to clean it up."

15) "Let's talk about 9/11. The people who were responsible for murdering 3,000 Americans on 9/11 have not been brought to justice. They are Osama bin Laden, al Qaeda and their sponsors, the Taliban. They were in Afghanistan. And yet George Bush and John McCain decided in 2002 that we should take our eye off of Afghanistan so that we could invade and occupy a country that had absolutely nothing to do with 9/11."

16) "Here are the results of their policy. Osama bin Laden and his top leadership—the people who murdered 3000 Americans—have a safe-haven in northwest Pakistan, where they operate with such freedom of action that they can still put out hate-filled audiotapes to the outside world. That's the result of the Bush-McCain approach to the war on terrorism."

17) "We need not throw away 200 years of American jurisprudence while we fight terrorism. We need not choose between our most deeply-held values and keeping this nation safe."

ON GOD AND RELIGION

What I appreciate about my country is:

_____

_____

What I love about my state is:

_____

_____

What I am grateful for about my city/town is:

_____

_____

What I am joyful about my family/fellowship/friends is:

_____

_____

What I acknowledge for myself is:

_____

_____

The action I am willing to take today for my country/state/city/
town/family/fellowship/friends/myself is:

_____

_____

ON GOD AND RELIGION

1) "We worship an awesome God in the Blue States, and we don't like federal agents poking around our libraries in the Red States. We coach Little League in the Blue States and have gay friends in the Red States."

2) "What I value most about Pastor Wright is not his day-to-day political advice. He's much more of a sounding board for me to make sure that I am speaking as truthfully about what I believe as possible and that I'm not losing myself in some of the hype and hoopla and stress that's involved in national politics."

3) "You know, my faith is one that admits some doubt."

4) "I was drawn to the power of the African-American religious tradition to spur social change. Out of necessity, the black church had to minister to the whole person. Out of necessity, the black church rarely had the luxury of separating individual salvation from collective salvation. It had to serve as the center of the community's political, economic, and social, as well as spiritual, life; it understood in an intimate way the biblical call to feed the hungry and clothe the naked and challenge powers and principalities. In the history of these struggles, I was able to see faith as more than just a comfort to the weary or a hedge against death; rather, it was an active, palpable agent in the world."

5) "This notion that's peddled by the religious right—that they are oppressed—is not true. Sometimes it's a cynical ploy to move their agenda ahead. The classic example being that somehow secularists are trying to eliminate Christmas, which strikes me as some kind of manufactured controversy."

6) "Our law is by definition a codification of morality; much of it grounded in the Judeo-Christian tradition."

ON GOD AND RELIGION

What I appreciate about my country is:

_____

_____

What I love about my state is:

_____

_____

What I am grateful for about my city/town is:

_____

_____

What I am joyful about my family/fellowship/friends is:

_____

_____

What I acknowledge for myself is:

_____

_____

The action I am willing to take today for my country/state/city/town/family/fellowship/friends/myself is:

_____

_____

ON GOD AND RELIGION—CONTINUED

7) "Faith doesn't mean that you don't have doubts."

8) "Faith is not just something you have, it's something you do."

9) "We should never forget that God granted us the power to reason so that we would do His work here on Earth—so that we would use science to cure disease, and heal the sick, and save lives."

10) "Like no other illness, AIDS tests our ability to put ourselves in someone else's shoes—to empathize with the plight of our fellow man. While most would agree that the AIDS orphan or the transfusion victim or the wronged wife contracted the disease through no fault of their own, it has too often been easy for some to point to the unfaithful husband or the promiscuous youth or the gay man and say, 'This is your fault. You have sinned.' I don't think that's a satisfactory response. My faith reminds me that we all are sinners."

11) "In the end, no amount of American forces can solve the political differences that lie at the heart of somebody else's civil war."

12) "I believe in the redemptive death and resurrection of Jesus Christ."

ON NATIONAL SECURITY

What I appreciate about my country is:

_____

_____

What I love about my state is:

_____

_____

What I am grateful for about my city/town is:

_____

_____

What I am joyful about my family/fellowship/friends is:

_____

_____

What I acknowledge for myself is:

_____

_____

The action I am willing to take today for my country/state/city/town/family/fellowship/friends/myself is:

_____

_____

ON NATIONAL SECURITY

1) "When we think of the major threats to our national security, the first to come to mind are nuclear proliferation, rogue states, and global terrorism. But another kind of threat lurks beyond our shores, one from nature, not humans—an avian flu pandemic."

2) "Let's talk about 9/11. The people who were responsible for murdering 3,000 Americans on 9/11 have not been brought to justice. They are Osama bin Laden, al Qaeda and their sponsors—the Taliban. They were in Afghanistan. And yet George Bush and John McCain decided in 2002 that we should take our eye off of Afghanistan so that we could invade and occupy a country that had absolutely nothing to do with 9/11."

3) "Here are the results of their policy: Osama bin Laden and his top leadership—the people who murdered 3000 Americans— have a safe-haven in northwest Pakistan, where they operate with such freedom of action that they can still put out hate-filled audiotapes to the outside world. That's the result of the Bush-McCain approach to the war on terrorism."

4) "We need not throw away 200 years of American jurisprudence while we fight terrorism. We need not choose between our most deeply-held values and keeping this nation safe."

5) "I refuse to be lectured on national security by people who are responsible for the most disastrous set of foreign policy decisions in the recent history of the United States."

ON OPPORTUNITY

What I appreciate about my country is:

_____

_____

What I love about my state is:

_____

_____

What I am grateful for about my city/town is:

_____

_____

What I am joyful about my family/fellowship/friends is:

_____

_____

What I acknowledge for myself is:

_____

_____

The action I am willing to take today for my country/state/city/
town/family/fellowship/friends/myself is:

_____

_____

ON OPPORTUNITY

1) "I have seen the desperation and disorder of the powerless: how it twists the lives of children on the streets of Jakarta or Nairobi in much the same way as it does the lives of children on Chicago's South Side; how narrow the path is for them between humiliation and untrammeled fury; how easily they slip into violence and despair."

2) "Whether chance of birth or circumstance decides life's big winners and losers, or whether we build a community where, at the very least, everyone has a chance to work hard, get ahead, and reach their dreams."

3) "Change will not come if we wait for some other person or some other time. We are the ones we've been waiting for. We are the change that we seek."

4) "I don't want to pit Red America against Blue America. I want to be President of the United States of America."

5) "Hope is what led a band of colonists to rise up against an empire; what led the greatest of generations to free a continent and heal a nation; what led young women and young men to sit at lunch counters and brave fire hoses and march through Selma and Montgomery for freedom's cause. Hope is what led me here today—with a father from Kenya, a mother from Kansas, and a story that could only happen in the United States of America. Hope is the bedrock of this nation; the belief that our destiny will not be written for us, but by us; by all those men and women who are not content to settle for the world as it is; who have courage to remake the world as it should be."

41

ON THE ENVIRONMENT/HELPING OTHERS

What I appreciate about my country is:

_____

_____

What I love about my state is:

_____

_____

What I am grateful for about my city/town is:

_____

_____

What I am joyful about my family/fellowship/friends is:

_____

_____

What I acknowledge for myself is:

_____

_____

The action I am willing to take today for my country/state/city/
town/family/fellowship/friends/myself is:

_____

_____

ON THE ENVIRONMENT

1) "All across the world, in every kind of environment and region known to man, increasingly dangerous weather patterns and devastating storms are abruptly putting an end to the long-running debate over whether or not climate change is real. Not only is it real, it's here, and its effects are giving rise to a frighteningly new global phenomenon: the man-made natural disaster."

ON HELPING THE LESS FORTUNATE

1) "We live in a culture that discourages empathy. A culture that too often tells us our principal goal in life is to be rich, thin, young, famous, safe, and entertained."

2) "You know, there's a lot of talk in this country about the federal deficit. But I think we should talk more about our empathy deficit—the ability to put ourselves in someone else's shoes; to see the world through the eyes of those who are different from us—the child who's hungry, the steelworker who's been laid-off, the family who lost the entire life they built together when the storm came to town. When you think like this—when you choose to broaden your ambit of concern and empathize with the plight of others, whether they are close friends or distant strangers—it becomes harder not to act; harder not to help."

ON THE ECONOMY/ON IMMIGRATION

What I appreciate about my country is:

_____

_____

What I love about my state is:

_____

_____

What I am grateful for about my city/town is:

_____

_____

What I am joyful about my family/fellowship/friends is:

_____

_____

What I acknowledge for myself is:

_____

_____

The action I am willing to take today for my country/state/city/
town/family/fellowship/friends/myself is:

_____

_____

ON THE ECONOMY

1) "When people are judged by merit, not connections, then the best and brightest can lead the country; people will work hard, and the entire economy will grow. Everyone will benefit and more resources will be available for all, not just select groups."

2) "The evangelists' success points to a hunger for the product they are selling; a hunger that goes beyond any particular issue or cause. They need an assurance that somebody out there cares about them; is listening to them."

ON IMMIGRATION

1) "I think the American people have a generous instinct. They understand that we're a nation of immigrants. But if those folks are going to live in this country, they have to be put on a pathway to citizenship that involves them paying a fine, making sure that they are at the back of the line and not cutting in front of people who applied legally to come into the country."

2) "Everybody knows politics is a contact sport."

ON NUCLEAR PROLIFERATION

What I appreciate about my country is:

_____

_____

What I love about my state is:

_____

_____

What I am grateful for about my city/town is:

_____

_____

What I am joyful about my family/fellowship/friends is:

_____

_____

What I acknowledge for myself is:

_____

_____

The action I am willing to take today for my country/state/city/
town/family/fellowship/friends/myself is:

_____

_____

ON NUCLEAR PROLIFERATION

1) "The single biggest threat that we face is a nuclear weapon or some weapon of mass destruction. What that means is that we have to be extraordinarily aggressive and vigilant in controlling nuclear proliferation."

2) "We have a nuclear proliferation treaty and strategy that has failed. I think it failed in Iran. It also failed in North Korea. That has to be rewritten and renegotiated."

3) "I am convinced that whenever we exaggerate or demonize, oversimplify or overstate our case, we lose."

4) "They say I need to be seasoned; they say I need to be stewed. They say, 'We need to boil all the hope out of him—like us—and then he'll be ready.'"

ON POLITICS

What I appreciate about my country is:

_____

_____

What I love about my state is:

_____

_____

What I am grateful for about my city/town is:

_____

_____

What I am joyful about my family/fellowship/friends is:

_____

_____

What I acknowledge for myself is:

_____

_____

The action I am willing to take today for my country/state/city/
town/family/fellowship/friends/myself is:

_____

_____

ON POLITICS

1) "The pursuit of ideological purity, the rigid orthodoxy, and the sheer predictability of our current political debate, that keeps us from finding new ways to meet the challenges we face as a country."

2) "What keeps us locked in 'either/or' thinking: the notion that we can only have big government or no government; the assumption that we must either tolerate forty-six million without health insurance or embrace 'socialized medicine.'"

3) "Politics has become so bitter and partisan, so gummed up by money and influence, that we can't tackle the big problems that demand solutions. And that's what we have to change first. We have to change our politics and come together around our common interests and concerns as Americans."

4) "We've gotta restore the American people's confidence in the ethics process by ensuring that political self-interest can no longer prevent politicians from enforcing ethics rules."

5) "The decisions that have been made in Washington these past six years, and the problems that have been ignored, have put our country in a precarious place."

49

ON POLITICS

What I appreciate about my country is:

_____

_____

What I love about my state is:

_____

_____

What I am grateful for about my city/town is:

_____

_____

What I am joyful about my family/fellowship/friends is:

_____

_____

What I acknowledge for myself is:

_____

_____

The action I am willing to take today for my country/state/city/
town/family/fellowship/friends/myself is:

_____

_____

ON POLITICS—CONTINUED

6) "Most people who meet my wife quickly conclude that she is remarkable. She is smart, funny, and thoroughly charming. Often, after hearing her speak at some function or working with her on a project, people will approach me and say something to the effect of, 'you know, I think the world of you, Barack, but your wife, wow!'"

7) "My belief in terms of moving forward on the ethics legislation is that we've got some low-hanging fruit that we should take care of right away."

8) "The internet today is an open platform where the demand for websites and services dictates success."

9) "We can't have a situation in which the corporate duopoly dictates the future of the internet and that's why I'm supporting what is called net neutrality."

10) "I think the American people, at their core, are a decent people."

11) "I think that we still have prejudice in our midst but I think that the vast majority of Americans are willing to judge people on the basis of, you know, their ideas and their character."

ON POLITICS

What I appreciate about my country is:

_____

_____

What I love about my state is:

_____

_____

What I am grateful for about my city/town is:

_____

_____

What I am joyful about my family/fellowship/friends is:

_____

_____

What I acknowledge for myself is:

_____

_____

The action I am willing to take today for my country/state/city/
town/family/fellowship/friends/myself is:

_____

_____

ON POLITICS—CONTINUED

12) "Hope—Hope in the face of difficulty. Hope in the face of uncertainty. The audacity of hope! In the end, that is God's greatest gift to us; the bedrock of this nation. A belief in things not seen. A belief that there are better days ahead."

13) "While there are few guarantees in life, you should be able to count on a job that pays the bills; health care for when you need it; a pension for when you retire; an education for your children that will allow them to fulfill their God-given potential. That's the America we believe in. That's the America I know."

14) "We think of faith as a source of comfort and understanding but find our expression of faith sowing division; we believe ourselves to be a tolerant people even as racial, religious, and cultural tensions roil the landscape. And instead of resolving these tensions or mediating these conflicts, our politics fans them, exploits them, and drives us further apart."

15) "We paint our faces red or blue and cheer our side and boo their side, and if it takes a late hit or cheap shot to beat the other team, so be it, for winning is all that matters. But I don't think so."

16) "Security and opportunity; compassion and prosperity aren't liberal values or conservative values—they're American values."

17) "It's not just enough to change the players. We've gotta change the game."

ON POLITICS

What I appreciate about my country is:

_____

_____

What I love about my state is:

_____

_____

What I am grateful for about my city/town is:

_____

_____

What I am joyful about my family/fellowship/friends is:

_____

_____

What I acknowledge for myself is:

_____

_____

The action I am willing to take today for my country/state/city/
town/family/fellowship/friends/myself is:

_____

_____

ON POLITICS—CONTINUED

18) "My wife has been my closest friend, my closest advisor. And...she's not somebody who looks to the limelight, or even is wild about me being in politics. And that's a good reality check on me. When I go home, she wants me to be a good father and a good husband. And everything else is secondary to that."

19) "Across America, a constant cross-pollination is occurring, a not-entirely-orderly but generally peaceful collision among people and cultures."

20) "Nothing can stand in the way of the power of millions of voices calling for change."

21) "America, this is our moment. This is our time. Our time to turn the page of the policies of the past."

22) "I honor—we honor—the service of John McCain, and I respect his many accomplishments, even if he chooses to deny mine."

23) "That's silly talk... Talk to my wife. She'll tell me I need to learn to just put my socks on the hamper."

24) "The decisions that have been made in Washington these past six years, and the problems that have been ignored, have put our country in a precarious place."

ON RACE

What I appreciate about my country is:

_____

_____

What I love about my state is:

_____

_____

What I am grateful for about my city/town is:

_____

_____

What I am joyful about my family/fellowship/friends is:

_____

_____

What I acknowledge for myself is:

_____

_____

The action I am willing to take today for my country/state/city/
town/family/fellowship/friends/myself is:

_____

_____

ON RACE

1) "The point I was making was not that my grandmother harbors any racial animosity. She doesn't. But she is a typical white person who, if she sees somebody on the street that she doesn't know, there's a reaction that's been bred into our experiences that don't go away, and that sometimes comes out in the wrong way, and that's just the nature of race in our society."

2) "We've got a tragic history when it comes to race in this country. We've got a lot of pent-up anger and bitterness and misunderstanding. This country wants to move beyond these kinds of things."

3) "But the anger is real; it is powerful; and to simply wish it away, to condemn it without understanding its roots, only serves to widen the chasm of misunderstanding that exists between the races."

4) "Nobody's suffering more than the Palestinian people from this whole process. And I would like to see—if we could get some movement from Palestinian leadership—what I'd like to see is a loosening up of some of the restrictions on providing aid directly to the Palestinian people."

ALSO BY CARL "TUCHY" PALMIERI:

The Platinum Rule and Other Contrarian Sayings
(BookSurge, 2006)

Tuchy's Law and Other Contrarian Quotes to Help You In Life's
Journey
(BookSurge, 2007)

Off The Wall Contrarian Quotes For People In Recovery
(BookSurge, 2007)

The Food Contrarian: Quotes for People Recovering From or
Dealing With Eating Issues
(BookSurge, 2007)

The Godsons
(BookSurge, 2007)

Josephine, In Her Words: Our Mom
(BookSurge, 2007)

Phil, In His Words: Our Dad
(BookSurge, 2007)

Relationship Magic
(BookSurge, 2008)

ALSO BY CARL "TUCHY" PALMIERI:

Money And So Much More: The True Meaning of Wealth
(BookSurge, 2008)

Sex and Intimacy: The Gifts of Life
(BookSurge, 2008)

When Man Listens: Everyone Can Listen to God
by Cecil Rose, reprinted by Carl "Tuchy" Palmieri
(BookSurge, 2008)

Relationship Recovery
(BookSurge, 2008)

Oprah, In Her Words: Our American Princess
(BookSurge, 2008)

The Conversion of the Church
by Sam Shoemaker, reprinted by Carl "Tuchy" Palmieri
(BookSurge, 2008)

Satisfying Success: And the Ways to Achieve It
(BookSurge, 2009)

ABOUT THE AUTHOR

Carl "Tuchy" Palmieri was born in 1942 in an old mansion belonging to the former mill owner of the factory where his father worked. His family was one of six related families that occupied the mansion. The second son of Italian immigrants, Carl grew up in Westport, Connecticut. After receiving a bachelor's degree in business administration from the University of Bridgeport he began his career marketing and installing accounting computers for the Burroughs Corporation. Twenty-one years later, in 1987, he started his own computer business. Carl is also the author of a series of self-help books.

Today Carl lives with his wife, Susan, in Fairfield, Connecticut. He has three children, two stepchildren, and 12 grandchildren. His nickname, Tuchy, comes from having been one of three Carls in his family. There was a "Big Carl," a "Carl the Twin," and "Carluch," which meant "Little Carl." "Carluch" evolved into "Carlatuch," "Tuch," and finally, "Tuchy."

www.ingramcontent.com/pod-product-compliance
Lightning Source LLC
Chambersburg PA
CBHW060645290526
45793CB00001B/405